The Thrill of Racing

LEE-ANNE T. SPALDING

Rourke
Publishing LLC
Vero Beach, Florida 32964

www.rourkepublishing.com

PHOTO CREDITS: © nicol ng heng lex: page 4; © Eldad Yitzhak: page 5; © Kawasaki Media: page 6, 14, 16; © HONDA MEDIA: PAGE 6; © KAREN KEAN: page 7; © Daniel Gustavsson: page 8, 9; © Alex Melnick: page 10; © Alan C. Heison: page 11; © Chrysler Media: page 12, 13; ©LandRover: page 13; © Kawasaki Media: page 14; © Gustavo Miguel Machado da Caridade Fernandes: page 15; ©Robynrg: page 16; © William Mahar: page 17; © Ford Media: page 18a,18b; © Luís Louro: page 19; © GM Media: page 20; © Yamaha Media: page 22;

Edited by Meg Greve
Cover and interior design by Tara Raymo

Library of Congress Cataloging-in-Publication Data

Spalding, Lee-Anne T.

Off-road racing / Lee-Anne T. Spalding.

    p. cm. -- (The thrill of racing)

Includes index.

ISBN 978-1-60472-376-2

1. Off-road racing--Juvenile literature. 2. Off-road vehicles--Juvenile

literature. I. Title.

GV1037.S72 2009

796.72--dc22

2008011249

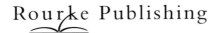

Rourke Publishing

www.rourkepublishing.com – rourke@rourkepublishing.com
Post Office Box 3328. Vero Beach. FL 32964

Table of Contents

When the Dirt First Flew

The adventure! The dirt! The edge! The **extreme** competition! Off-road racing has been around since the early 1900s. Drivers of **modified** vehicles like trucks, cars, motorcycles, and buggies race on natural **terrain** such as mud, sand, and rocks.

Ed Pearlman formed the National Off-Road Racing Association (NORRA) in 1967. Since then, many types of organized races have occurred on natural terrain and temporary tracks constructed for **stadium** racing.

OFF-ROAD FIRSTS

	1913
1920s	International Six Days Enduro
Desert racing events	
	1967
1970s	Pearlman forms NORRA
Mud bogging events	
	1978
	First Dakar Rally

Thrilling Fact

In some remote parts of the world, off-road driving is the typical form of transportation. Unpaved roads and harsh terrain require people to off-road in everyday travel.

Desert Racing

Desert racing requires drivers to race through a desert with their off-road vehicles. The vehicles may be motorcycles, dune buggies, trucks, or all terrain vehicles (ATVs). These races take place in deserts around the world.

The first off-road desert race occurred in Mexico. It is now known as the Baja 1000.

Two styles of desert races are the Loop Race and Point to Point. The Loop Race course, named for its shape, usually has racers traveling on dirt bikes up to 40 miles (64 kilometers) and completing at least two different loops. Point to point races test the endurance and skill of the driver. Often, these races are over 1,000 miles (1,609 kilometers) in length. They begin and end in two different places.

A Safe Ride

A sandrail is a type of dune buggy built with a roll cage which requires a whip antenna. The antenna must be at least eight feet (2.4 meters) long so that racers can avoid collisions as they **maneuver** through the sand dunes.

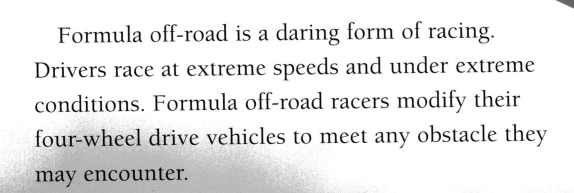

Formula off-road is a daring form of racing. Drivers race at extreme speeds and under extreme conditions. Formula off-road racers modify their four-wheel drive vehicles to meet any obstacle they may encounter.

Special wheels in off-road racing grip slippery terrain and keep the vehicle from flipping.

You Asked...

What does four-wheel drive mean?

It means that all four wheels on the vehicle work together to drive on natural terrain like mud, ice, or other slippery surfaces.

Formula off-road vehicles have a **secure** roll cage for their driver, special sand drag tires, and amazing suspension components. These shock absorbers enable the vehicles to jump higher and handle rough terrain.

Mud bogging, also known as mud racing, is a popular motorsport in the United States. The goal is to maneuver your four-wheel drive vehicle through a specific distance in mud. The winner of the race is the vehicle that makes it through the mud the fastest!

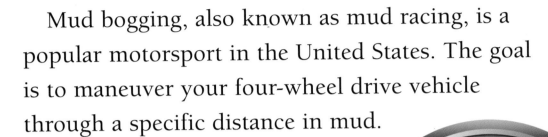

Thrilling Fact

Dennis Anderson's popular monster truck, Grave Digger was also a mud bogger.

There are many types of mud bogs. Hill and hole bogs are just as they sound: a series of hills and holes to challenge the vehicle and driver. Flat tracks are like drag strips or straight stretches of mud. Open bogs have little organization and occur naturally in our **environment**.

Rock crawling is an extreme form of off-road racing. Drivers maneuver their modified vehicles over harsh terrain like boulders, mountain foothills, rock piles, or mountain trails. For competition, obstacle courses range in distance from 100 to 200 feet (30 to 61 meters).

Caution: Danger Zone

Many rock climbing vehicles have a roll cage built around the whole driver for protection in case of roll overs.

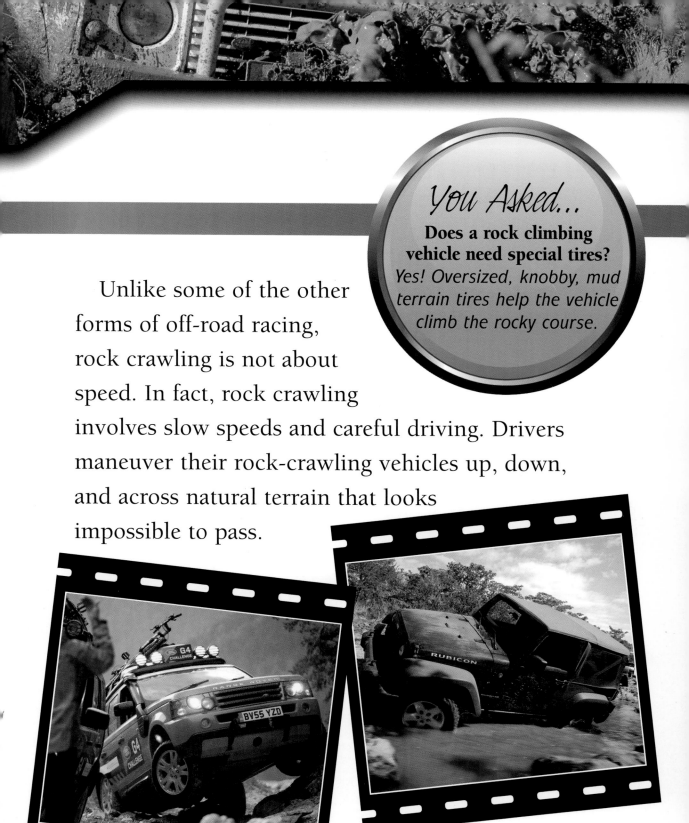

Unlike some of the other forms of off-road racing, rock crawling is not about speed. In fact, rock crawling involves slow speeds and careful driving. Drivers maneuver their rock-crawling vehicles up, down, and across natural terrain that looks impossible to pass.

Bikers race off-road motorcycles in a variety of events. Enduro is a type of off-road motorcycle racing that refers to the endurance of the rider and the machine. In the World Enduro Championship events, bikers race for two entire days.

Even bigger than enduros are cross-country rallies. Cross-country rallies take place over many days and many miles. Motorcycle riders can travel several hundred miles over open terrain. The most famous cross-country event is the Dakar Rally that takes riders almost two full weeks to complete.

The Dakar Rally begins in France and ends in Senegal.

Built to race, these four-wheeled machines allow drivers to perform single jumps and double jumps. Drivers race ATVs on sand, through the woods, and even on ice!

Thrilling Fact

In June of 2006, Terry Wilmeth set a world record of 149.4 miles per hour (240.4 kilometers per hour) for the highest speed ever achieved on an ATV.

Ice racing requires an ATV to cross frozen rivers or lakes. Cold weather is a requirement for natural ice, so these events usually take place in colder climates.

A four-wheeled ATV known as a quad bike, races across a frozen lake.

Four-Wheel Jamboree Nationals occur all over the United States each year for fans of mud bogging events. The International Six Days Enduro is the oldest off-road motorcycle event first held in England in 1913. The Dakar Rally is a desert racing event that has taken place since 1978. In southern California, the Baja 1000 has held an event since 1967 for desert racing vehicles of all kinds. Off-road racing opportunities seem to be endless.

Countries Which Host Off-Road Races

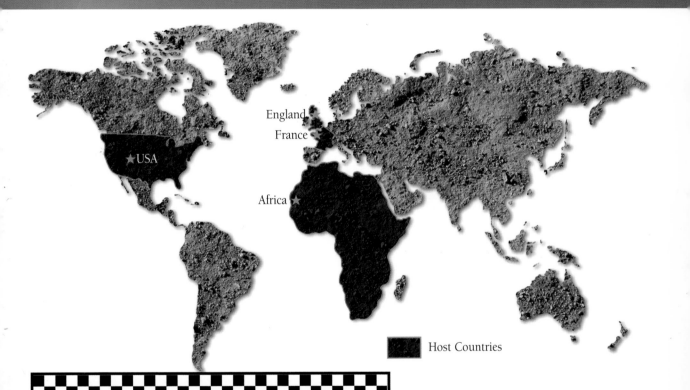

England
France
★USA
Africa ★

▮ Host Countries

Caution: Danger Zone

Booby traps, or hidden traps and obstacles, appear occasionally at off-road events. Well-meaning **spectators** sometimes create holes, hills or bury obstacles to add to their viewing pleasure.

The thrill of the race can be expensive. Mud bogging monster trucks can cost $150,000. New sandrail dune buggies cost anywhere from $20,000 to $100,000. The modifications made to the vehicles, which allow them to compete on off-road terrain, add up to thousands and thousands of dollars.

Average Price of Racing Gear

RACING GEAR	AVERAGE PRICE
Helmet	$200
Goggles	$35
Jersey	$35
Under-the-jersey chest protector	$60
Over-the-jersey chest protector	$120
Boots	$160
Pants	$100
Gloves	$30
Kidney belt	$30
Knee guards	$50
Elbow guards	$23
Wrist guards	$26
Neck guard	$30

Thrilling Fact

For top of the line racing gear, the prices add up. The grand total equals over $900!

Off-road racing events occur worldwide in many climates and over many terrains. Deserts, forests, rivers, lakes, and a whole lot of dirt make for exciting and heart pounding events. Whether you witness an off-road race in a stadium, like mud bogging at a monster truck event, or you see dune buggies flying over sand dunes in a desert race on television, off-road races are sure to give you a thrill!

Glossary

environment (en-VYE-ruhn-muhnt): the area or natural world which surrounds us

extreme (ek-STREEM): very great

maneuver (muh-NOO-ver): to move something carefully into a particular position

modified (MOD-uh-fyed): to change something slightly

secure (si-KYOOR): safe, firmly closed, or well protected

spectators (SPEK-tay-turs): people who watch an event

stadium (STAY-dee-uhm): a place where sporting events or races can be viewed by many

terrain (tuh-RAYN): ground or land

Index

Websites to Visit

http://familyevents.com

http://race.off-road.com/

http://en.wikipedia.org/wiki/Off-road_racing

Further Reading

Gifford, Clive. Racing: *The Ultimate Motorsports Encyclopedia*. Kingfisher, 2006.

Marks, Jennifer. *Dune Buggies*. Blazers, 2006.

Poolos, J. *Wild About ATVs*. Capstone Press, 2007.

About the Author

Lee-Anne Trimble Spalding is a former public school educator and is currently instructing preservice teachers at the University of Central Florida. She lives in Oviedo, Florida with her husband, Brett and two sons, Graham and Gavin.